ADULTING AS
A MILLENNIAL

Mindfully
Asher Tarby

ADULTING AS A MILLENNIAL

A GUIDE TO EVERYTHING YOUR PARENTS DIDN'T TEACH YOU

Asha Tarry, CLC, LMSW

Jones Media Publishing
10645 N. Tatum Blvd. Ste. 200-166
Phoenix, AZ 85028
www.JonesMediaPublishing.com

Disclaimer:

The author strives to be as accurate and complete as possible in the creation of this book, notwithstanding the fact that the author does not warrant or represent at any time that the contents within are accurate due to the rapidly changing nature of the Internet.

While all attempts have been made to verify information provided in this publication, the Author and the Publisher assume no responsibility and are not liable for errors, omissions, or contrary interpretation of the subject matter herein. The Author and Publisher hereby disclaim any liability, loss or damage incurred as a result of the application and utilization, whether directly or indirectly, of any information, suggestion, advice, or procedure in this book. Any perceived slights of specific persons, peoples, or organizations are unintentional.

In practical advice books, like anything else in life, there are no guarantees of income made. Readers are cautioned to rely on their own judgment about their individual circumstances to act accordingly. Readers are responsible for their own actions, choices, and results. This book is not intended for use as a source of legal, business, accounting or financial advice. All readers are advised to seek the services of competent professionals in legal, business, accounting, and finance field.

Printed in the United States of America

ISBN: 978-1-948382-02-1 paperback
JMP2020.1

DEDICATION

For my father, the man who helped
make me the woman I am today.

CONTENTS

Acknowledgements

I would like to thank my writing coach, Jeremy Jones of Jones Media Publishing, who guided me the entire way and cheered me on when I needed it. I would also like to thank my closest loved ones— my family and friends—who are there for me no matter what. I especially want to thank the people who have supported my work throughout the years. This book is for you!

Introduction

As someone who grew up on the cusp of a changing era, I have struggled with not only finding personal happiness but also trying to stop pleasing others in order to gain their approval. Being pulled apart like this is a feeling I know well. For millennials, I do not think it is much different than it was for my generation—Gen X—to want to live a life that not only makes you feel good about who you are but also leaves a lasting legacy for doing something great. However, the way millennials get to that life is quite different than how the boomers did it and definitely different from how we Gen Xers did it. Millennials are unique because they are willing to take risks more than any other generation. I find that admirable. At the same time, what is missing is the guidance from earlier generations, who have lived a little, to help millennials navigate the course of living life, including teaching them how to develop mental fitness and to appreciate and nurture mutually beneficial relationships..

When I was four years old, I told my parents I was going to be a nurse when I grew up. A nurse? What did I know about nursing? Nothing. But that is what I professed to them and was very certain I was going to become. Along the way, I worked hard to make this dream a reality. I worked hard at school, in a way. I mean, school sort of came easy to me until I went off to college, but I continued to at least learn, participate, and comply with what was expected of me. I also worked hard at being a good person, or at least that is what I believed I was doing.

I knew early in life that I liked how it felt to please others: from my parents to my teachers to all the other adults in between that I knew. That feeling of praise—a smile, a hug, a positive word—gave me a warm feeling inside. Eventually, I became conditioned to that feeling, and for a while it worked in my favor, or so I thought. As with everything else in life, that warm feeling changed, and as I got older and more in touch with my authentic self, I recognized how people pleasing can be a detriment to my well-being.

But first let me get back to becoming a nurse. I thought back then that helping people and getting paid for it would be the greatest thing ever! I would not only get to heal people but be able to teach people how to heal themselves, and, in turn, that would make me feel good about me. When I told my family, as well as my friends and their parents, that I was going to be a nurse when I grew up, they all lauded me for it. My dad would let me use him as a guinea pig: I took his pretend temperature, read him his pretend results, and patched up his pretend wounds. To this day, I still appreciate him for accommodating me the ways that he did. As a father he knew how important it was to me.

When I decided to enroll in college for nursing, I looked at a few schools on the East Coast that had high-performing programs, but when I began attending college tours, I found out that some of the schools I wanted to attend would not accept someone with lower than a twelve hundred on their SATs. I scored somewhere in the nine hundreds. I was a smart kid, but I was not a strong standardized test-taker. As I faced the beginning of multiple rejections from some of my top school choices, I was confronted by my parents' expectations and fears about my future.

During junior year of high school, I took a filmmaking class—to my surprise I really enjoyed it, so I enrolled in yet another elective course of acting and directing the following semester. Well, by the end of that school year, my teacher informed me that she added my name into a scholarship board for students in the performing arts to audition for a state scholarship in acting. I could not believe it—someone thought I was talented enough to pursue acting. Before then I had never thought of being anything else but a healthcare professional. Now, I had the opportunity to think that I could do something else, something that scared me as well as excited me and put spontaneity at the forefront of my work.

As I began wrapping my head around this newly discovered talent, I prepared two monologues with my teacher for the audition: a Shakespearean monologue and one of my choosing. After several weeks of rehearsing, the day finally came for my audition, and by then I was a ball of nerves. My dad and I rode silently to the place where I would be performing for acting directors for the very first time. I had already been a dancer for twelve years up to then, but as a dancer I did not have to communicate (at least not in words), so I was not sure how I would be received or what I would be judged on besides my performance. When I approached the door to the building of the audition, I began to feel a slow growing pain in the pit of my stomach. I walked inside and saw what appeared to be professionally trained teenagers doing voice exercises, breathing techniques, and stretching—I thought, "I'm not going to be able to do this!" I almost turned around and walked out, but then I thought, "What will I say to my father"— who was waiting in the car—"or to my friends at school or to my teacher, who had coached me for weeks?"

The time finally came when my number was called. I walked into a room with three stoic faces sitting behind a white table, all of them emitting the chill of an ice-cold cooler. I took a deep breath, exhaled, and visualized myself going all in; however, after reciting the first few lines, my brain went numb and I could not remember what I had previously rehearsed. I was suddenly stuck, in a slight panic: "What was I going to do?" I thought. "What would my teacher back at school say if I left without finishing?" If I failed the audition, that is it! No scholarship, no acting. I would have to go right back to thinking about nursing and I was not so sure I wanted to do that anymore. I took a deep breath, exhaled, and asked if I could begin again. Thankfully, the judges said yes. When I was done, I made a beeline for the door and out to the car where my dad was waiting for me. All I wanted was to get out of there and go back to my normal, mundane life.

As the weeks rolled by, I forgot about the audition and kept plugging away at the usual: classwork, friends, boys, homework, dance, and chores. Those things were pretty much my only focus for a while. Until one day at school, my teacher told me I was nominated for a fifteen-hundred-dollar scholarship for acting. My mind was completely blown. How was it possible that I was considered among the hundreds of talented people in the area to receive an award? Did they not remember I messed up? I could not even remember my lines after the first minute into my performance. Nevertheless, I was excited, happy, and anxious. I could not wait to tell my parents! That day after having dinner with my folks, I told my mother and father that I had been nominated for the scholarship in acting; if I chose to study performing arts in college, I would be awarded fifteen hundred dollars toward my academic career. Well, I cannot begin to tell you the reality check I got from them. I was barraged with questions about how I would earn a living after college and about my plans to become a nurse. They informed me that I would not receive any financial support if I pursued an acting career after high school—that was sobering. Being financially cut off at eighteen was not in my plans, so I reverted to the idea of becoming a professional helper. And that was that, at least for a while.

At one point, I was receptive to the idea of serendipity as the saving grace from the uniformity of my mundane life. But, I found that some things require focus and a plan. Actually, lots of things in life require several plans. I discovered that it was possible to do the things that I wanted to do, but I could do those things while also being responsible with my relationships, my health, and my money—or my parents' money, until I earned my own money and made my own financial decisions.

All of these things became prominent as I made mistakes and learned from those mistakes. You will make mistakes too. The earlier you accept that, the better off you will be and the more resilient you will become. The lessons I share in this book helped me to fall down without falling apart. My hope is that you will allow yourself to fall too and get back up. As many times as you can.

Believe in Yourself

When I was a young girl, I recall writing a letter to my aunt expressing how much I wanted to grow up and live in New York City. I wrote that I would travel the world, trying new things and taking on new adventures. I could literally see in my mind what that would be like.

Years later when I became an adult, she reminded me of that letter and returned to it several times throughout our conversations. She was tickled by the idea that I had such a vivid imagination and spoke so matter-of-fact about my future from such an early age. I do not know why, but I had a feeling and a mindset that led me to believe that I could do anything. To this day, I continue to talk with certainty about my life.

So many times in high school I used to fantasize about the things I wanted to do after graduation. I used to dream about the people I wanted to meet and the places I wanted to go: my mind was a fertile ground for ideas. I did not tell many people back then what I was thinking, but every now and then when a friend's parent asked about my plans for the future, I would say, "Well, I'm going to college in New York." I did not hesitate or stutter. I said it at thirteen years old like I was already a grown-up with an inheritance and a backpack ready to follow my hopes and dreams. I am not sure how I learned to think and speak that way, but a part of me now believes it may have had something to do with these Les Brown videos I used to watch with my father.

When I was growing up, the American speaker Les Brown was the first black man I had ever seen on television who spoke with such candor about his childhood and who exuded so much confidence in his abilities. He used humor to hold his audience's attention when he told his powerful anecdotes. I used to sit at my dad's feet beside his favorite chair in my parents' bedroom, watching Les Brown move crowds of people with his moving imagery. I began to look forward to these moments with my father and Les Brown. I was drawn to this man like a child to their favorite icon. I cannot remember exactly what he said that influenced me, but as early as eleven or twelve years old, I dreamed an impossible dream, believing and knowing that I could make it come true. Not long after that I began speaking and behaving in ways that mirrored that type of thinking.

Occasionally, my mother would confront me with questions about my future, such as

"How do you think you're going to afford an apartment in New York City?" At the time, we were living in a two-story house in southern Maryland in a middle-income community, following a transition we made from New York to the suburbs years earlier. My mother said, "New York is expensive, and we do not have money for you to go to school there. Who's going to pay for that?" Though my grades were good, my first round of SAT scores were only fair; incidentally, because she did not share my vision, it came across as her doubting me. Today, I think it was fear: she was afraid because although she had defied a lot of obstacles too, her parents could never dream up the life my mom came to live. She had done some extraordinary things not only in her life but also in her career. I believe she thought I was different than she was. Instead, what I believe is that we are both rebels. I was a modern-day thinker with big goals and far less fear than she tried to instill in me. That was okay. I did not know it then, but everything would work itself out. I just needed training in developing a thick skin first.

Often, I was told by people that I was introverted and sensitive; however, if I was going to make life as extraordinary as I saw it could be, I had to become somewhat desensitized to criticism. From then on, I kept most of my plans to myself and just quietly executed those visions I initially talked about—for example, when I imagined where I wanted to go to college, I would visualize myself there in my mind first. I would do this over and over in my head. Or, when I dreamed about the place I would live upon graduating, I would visually transport myself through time into the beautifully designed and decorated home I would purchase just for me. When I thought about the people I wanted to meet and work with, I would once again imagine myself speaking with confidence to them whenever we would meet. In doing this mental work I noticed the visceral reactions

I would experience. It was pure excitement: adrenaline that I lived for.

I repeated these practices to myself day in and day out, without sharing what I was doing with doubters. I only talked about my visions when I thought it necessary or to people who also carried a transformative energy, radical thinking, and the mindset of turning dreams into reality. Though I used visual imagery, fantasies, and affirming language, I worked consistently on myself so that I could be ready to handle the things I was looking forward to. Taking these steps elevated my personal drive and, subsequently, the people and places I later became acquainted with.

I did not have a coach or a mentor at the time. I was still an adolescent. I also did not know what those things were back then, but I knew I needed a plan, some time, a lot of focus, and inspiration. How I was going to get all of that was beside the point, but I knew I needed to stay on course.

Around the tenth grade I started to read more books. I met a few friends from freshmen year who were like-minded thinkers and doers, and together we banded and began swapping authors and ideas. Back then we had a small Black student union which I was not yet a member of, but I figured I had better join so I could start getting my name out there (early branding I suppose). I also needed the experience of directing and producing. (Again, this at the time from the mind of a sixteen-year-old.) I cannot remember the position I held in the student union, but the most important thing I do recall was how magnificent it felt when the teacher that oversaw us gave the members the greenlight to produce the first Black History Month program, consisting of poetry, dance, and music.

That year my classmates and I put on the best show that school had ever seen. We covered a few of the most prominent times in American history, showcasing art, literature, and social justice from the Harlem Renaissance to the Black Power Movement. We had a talented tap dancer from my class perform a unique piece, accompanied by a trained pianist from one of the upper classes. We had some of the female students in my class portray powerful women in the Black Panther Party who often went uncredited, such as Assata Shakur, Kathleen Cleaver, and Elaine Brown. It was one magical hour of entertainment and education. To this day, I can close my eyes and still feel what that day was like. That moment was the beginning of how I wanted to feel doing something I loved—I wanted to create; I wanted to produce; I wanted to do things that made me feel alive.

Purpose was the first life lesson I learned about. I learned that you must be mindful of what you are receiving, both visually and audibly. It is critical too that you have at least one person in your circle who is also self-developing and excited about renewing their mind. My dad was an old man when we used to sit together at night watching Les Brown seminars on television. But, it was through modeling my father's behavior that I saw how important it is to continue learning as you age. My dad was also willing to listen to other perspectives. His mind was ripe well into his eighties. He was my first inspiration and my first mentor—and this book is dedicated to him.

* * *

What are you actively doing each day to renew your mind? How does it make you feel when you do those things? This book is going to help you create mindful steps toward living a life of purpose. The goal is to help you notice how many things you have already done, which may lead you to become intentional about your life and to do things mindfully, even when you think the gesture is so small that it will not make a difference. It will.

At the end of this book I want you to feel inspired to create a life worth living intentionally, by your own design, with more joy, more meaning, and exponentially more love.

It's Not Always about You and That's a Good Thing

Before I graduated high school, I had been accepted to two of the three colleges I had applied to: Delaware State University and Pace University. I chose Pace University in Pleasantville, New York, foremost because I was going back home, which was the first dream I manifested. And second, because I received almost 50 percent in scholarship money toward tuition and campus housing. I do not think my parents ever thought I would attend the college of my choosing, but I did. By the end of summer, I was off to school and to a host of unexpected new beginnings.

But, after two years of studying nonstop for my clinical nursing courses, I came to realize how much I did not enjoy the nursing program. I dedicated lots of hours to independent and group studies but could barely maintain my grades at the standard I was used to. The more I tried, the more I seemed to despise how hard I was working without seeing the results of my intense labor. I studied before school, and sometimes during my breaks; I studied at the end of my day, into the late hours of the night practically every day, sometimes falling asleep on top of my books. Still, I did not get why I could not excel in this program the way I did in high school.

Finally, the straw that broke my back was when I finished the last round of spring finals: I went to the community board to read my previous week's test scores for Anatomy & Physiology II, and I learned that I missed the minimum required score to be promoted to the next level of nursing for the following school year ("What, I did not pass?"). Not passing during the spring semester meant I would have to repeat my entire year over, starting the next year's spring semester—and I was not about to do that. I was angry. Furious, actually. I was also very, very tired and I felt a little hopeless. All these months of sacrificing my social life and giving up sleep, plus adding twenty extra pounds to the scale, and I still did not pass the exam? It took a little time to sink in, but I was able to see how unhappy I had been those past two years. I really did not enjoy what I was doing as much as I enjoyed telling people what I was in school for. There is always a subject or a career path that makes people envy you or respect your determination. But, that did not matter to me anymore. Instead, I cared about how I was getting by. I cared about how tired I felt and how I had little interest in what I was studying at times. On top of that, the early clinical practicum hours at the nursing home—where sometimes angry patients said obnoxious things and incontinent patients unfortunately could not keep their bowels from spilling over after you cleaned them several times—was not quite the life I had imagined for myself decades earlier.

Thankfully, the universe was guiding me and preparing me for things that would lead me closer to my destiny. I did not know what to expect in the beginning and I surely did not think I would get what I got. I just knew that I did not want to be behind my prospective graduating class nor want to tell my parents that I might drop out of school, so I called my best friend, Melissa, and told her what happened. She suggested I take a class in her major, Human Services, and I did; I registered for two classes. I figured that if I am going to stay in school, then I will give it all I have got one more time before I change my mind. I have learned over the years that if you are going to transform yourself, you must let go of the negative experiences you have had in the past and clear your mind of whatever let downs you have had so that you can embrace the abundant things that will come your way. I committed to making this work.

I liked that Human Services was still in the helping industry, and according to Melissa, I probably would not lose any of the credits I had gained in my other courses because the credits still applied to the requirements I needed for both majors. I was back on track. I confirmed Melissa's guess about the credits; the registrar's office said I would not lose any time I earned for the previous classes I had already passed. I then mentally tasked myself with being open to learning and doing my best work again. I showed up early for school each time I was expected to be in class. I raised my hand to ask questions and gave feedback. I studied for my exams like I had always. By the end of the semester, in Human Behavior I & II I received an A and a B+ respectively.

It was a no brainer after that to declare Human Services my new major. This was the easiest decision I made in college. I thought it was smooth sailing from then on. However, there was much more to learn about who I was becoming. And what was in store was nothing close to what I would have thought I needed to know.

Shortly after making the decision to change my major, the interim department chair informed me that my academic record would have to be approved by the queen of all academic queens, Dr. Marie Werner: a badass instructor whose reputation preceded her and who would have the last say as to whether I was on my way to becoming a graduate or a once-upon-a-time Pace University student. At the start of that summer leading into my junior year, I also discovered that I had to complete a three-month internship as a requirement for matriculation into the program. I was back in Maryland by then and uncertain about the future again, when the very first conversation with my new adviser and professor of most of the Human Services courses went rogue. At the time, I did not have a clue who Dr. Werner was, but I heard she was a no-nonsense woman who was serious about her craft. I soon came to find out that she was also a passionate PhD-level social worker, with a tremendous mind and high standards: she was a warrior woman.

My introduction to Dr. Werner was over the telephone, and it was not the same initial impression that everyone else had of her. When we spoke, she was curt and more matter-of-fact than I expected. After she disclosed why, I was able to sympathize with her but not before taking her shortness personally. You see, what I did not know at first was that Dr. Werner was going through a major life transition of her own, one that would take her life in a direction she too could not have possibly prepared for. When I planned the call, I thought I was going to receive guidance on what next steps to take in my academic career, instead what I received was a lesson on being present, present to the only moments we have. The *now* puts even the slightest thing into context; the *now* makes other things, including your own fear, seem insignificant in the bigger scheme of things. Most importantly, being mindful of what is going on in yourself is not the focus of everyone else, because everyone is experiencing each moment separate from you.

Dr. Werner was facing the battle of her life. After trying to hold it together for a few moments following my barrage of inquiries, she blurted out, "I'm sorry to be so short with you, but I was just diagnosed with cancer!" My heart dropped down into my stomach. I had no words to give. I could not describe at all how I felt in that moment. I did not know her well enough to start asking questions about it. All I initially wanted when I called was to get my questions answered about the internship and move on to the next thing on my to-do list. In retrospect, I do not even remember thinking to ask her anything about herself. What I recall is leaping into a monologue about my past failures and my present fears, and I expected her to help me through it. Maybe.

I had not considered that she too is a person with a life of her own; then, I suddenly learned that she was living with a serious health crisis and other things outside of work. Also, she was taking my call during what was her summer break to help me out. It took a while to realize this, but that day changed my entire perspective about humanity. I am not the center of it all: not me nor anyone else. This was a lesson I would repeatedly connect with throughout my journey of self-discovery. I then began to feel sad for her and less anxious within myself because I knew I would eventually have everything I needed.

Once again, I did not know how, but I trusted that I would figure it out.

Fortunately, as with most things I have learned after that conversation with Dr. Werner, life will eventually make things clear. I needed not only to pace myself a little more and connect to what was going on inside of me those past few years in college but also to start thinking about how to build connections with people who could help me. Throughout this book, you will see that everything is interconnected—from who we meet to what we do to when we get the lesson and how we get it.

I was fortunate enough to meet Dr. Werner in person that next semester. She returned to Pace just a few months after her diagnosis, but this time when we met face-to-face, we had history. We had regard for one another. And I had a new understanding of who I was becoming. I was part of a greater perspective other than my own. And in accepting that, I began to do things with more intention than I had previously.

* * *

Are you receptive to discovering who you are becoming even if that means it does not look exactly how you saw it in your mind? How many times have you wanted to give up because the outcome was different than you expected? Well, if so, that is alright. Hopefully, you recognize what that time was for—or at least that that time had a purpose, although you may not always know why. But one day, I believe you will.

How are you using your five senses to demonstrate what you are experiencing? For example, what do you notice about how you absorb and interpret information? Do you think of only the negative experiences you've had as failures or as lessons? Are your feelings dictating what you do again or what you stop doing, such as pursuing your goals? Look for the evidence to this question.

Remember this—we all have a purpose. Yet, getting to know what our purpose is might include going through some unexpected events; you might go places and meet people along the way that are there to help you get out of your way. Do you notice them? That is what has happened to me and to so many others. It is who you meet along the way to becoming who you are meant to be that shows you who you are. It is also about staying committed to your commitments that keep you grounded: commit to not giving up so easily, commit to being patient for an affirming outcome to arrive, commit to not going along this journey by yourself. Be willing to let go of the stories you have or make up about what is not working. Our lives are to be lived, although at times you do not know what is coming next. The process of being in the moment is all you have. What you do with each moment is up to you—but remember, every moment is not just about you.

Doing It Anyway

In the last chapter I talked about how empathy has informed my principles: the beliefs and practices about the ways I show up in the world. The second important life lesson is about committing to one's commitments. Your words and actions say a lot about how you cope with adversity We all have things we want to do, yet sometimes we either make excuses about not doing them or we procrastinate and avoid getting started. As soon as I began to recognize that what I want starts with how deeply committed I am to the commitment, I developed a no-matter-what-it-takes attitude and got to work. It took some discipline of course, but more importantly, it took commitment to reaching my goals that helped me accomplish most of them.

In the book *The ONE Thing* by Gary Keller and Jay Papasan (2012), the authors state that success is not necessarily about being disciplined but rather "choosing the right habit and bringing just enough discipline to it to establish the right habit. Without that we get frustrated and give up." I agree. Too often when we do not see results, or at least the results we hoped for, we tend to feel defeated. Defeatism then translates into how we start treating the necessary habits for success. I do not always feel like performing the right actions in order to get the thing I want to get, but that is okay. It does not matter that much how I feel. Instead for me, it matters that I tell myself the truth and stick with what I have set out to do. How often have you said to yourself you would do something, but then you let other things take priority over them? How does it feel to do that?

Sometimes I wonder if some of us believe that success involves having constant affirmation from teams of people around you cheering you on toward the finish line. Successful people are successful because they recognize that although a dream may begin with a feeling, it does not remain a feeling: it becomes a purpose, a purpose that drives them every day to get up and commit to the actions that will produce something great; in essence, it is their commitment to a greater purpose that leads to their achievement. I think if I did not put so much value into my word, I may have dropped the ball on a lot of things I planned to do. Our minds are partly to blame for that.

Ordinarily, our brains want to make things easy so that when we tell ourselves to do things in a way that challenges us to think new thoughts and create new patterns of programming, we may notice how difficult it is to change those old habits. Not all human beings are innately motivated. Motivational speaking is one of the most illustrious industries out there, mostly because those who do it know that people do not wake up motivated. They turn on the motivation in order to complete their goals and that requires affirming thoughts, inspiring sounds and visuals, a healthy attitude, and a commitment to getting stuff done. How someone feels about it every day is not all that matters: feelings are not facts but rather feedback. If we pay attention to the feedback, feelings will also teach us what we need to do to keep us doing the thing that matters most: our purpose.

Notice that I said a "healthy attitude," not a positive one, because I do not believe we need to feel positive all the time. Sometimes, the most profound lessons come from other experiences we have with our emotions. Yet, I do however believe that having a healthy attitude involves recognizing what attitude you have about the thing you are accomplishing.

Every time I analyze the what and the why of my behavior, I start asking myself questions around whether those actions align with my purpose. When I study why I may be feeling a certain way, I begin to take stock of my role, my daily practices, my surroundings, and the people I am spending time with to see if there is something I must change in order to gain clarity and refocus. Whenever I inventory my feelings, I discover a lot of things about myself, some of which involves me changing my mindset as well as my routine. Doing so usually helps to maximize the likelihood of me reaching my goals on time. It is not always easy, but it is helpful.

In my work and relationships with millennials, I have seen how feeling optimistic and doing things that have meaning for them translates to their sticking with their goals. I have spent countless hours talking with millennials, critiquing their thinking, not because there is something wrong with optimism or desire, quite the contrary: those things are valuable to have. However, what is happening with these limiting beliefs is how operating in work, life, and relationships are reduced to one's feelings. That kind of existence creates distance between reality and idealism, which can be quite tragic if you believe that other people think exactly the way you think.

Remember what I said earlier about our brains: we want things to be simple and to feel good. How we develop more tolerance for things unlike ourselves is to develop intrigue, a willingness to learn from others, and patience to do both. Subsequently, that leads me to my next and most important life lesson about integrity.

Integrity has taught me a great deal about people. People will tell you what they will do, people will tell you what you want to hear, yet, people do not always consider how either makes the other think or feel. I have heard it said before that "people won't always remember what you say but they will remember how you made them feel." I took that to also mean that your most powerful moments will be remembered by what impression you gave about who you are.

My dad used to repeatedly say, "If you tell people you are going to do something, then do it. And if you change your mind, at least say something about it." Today, people just say whatever comes out of their mouth. A lot of times they do not hear themselves when they speak. They talk from their unwise mind and copy the things they see everyone else doing. Then, they worry about whether people notice them.

My question to you is: how do you want people to think of what you are presenting to the world? Does your word matter?

Words Count

Growing up I learned some of the most profound life lessons that have shaped the person I am today. In recent years, it has made me appreciate aspects of my childhood and the way I grew up more than I ever thought I could. I did not accept every lesson without resistance at times; however, those lessons are usually the ones you need and remember the most.

Starting with this lesson: when I was a teen, my parents drilled into me to soon follow through with doing something after I said I would do it. For example, my friends would call the house to talk with me. On the occasions I was unavailable, they would talk with my mother, who in turn would leave me a note telling me to call them back when I got the message. A lot of times when my mom saw me, after taking one of those messages from my friends, she would check in with me about my returning the call. Sometimes, I had already spoken to the friend by the time she asked. At other times, it took me a bit longer to get to it. Though most times I told her that I was going to do what I promised, she would stay on me until I did. If I did not, my father would occasionally give me a short lecture about it. This happened even when it was another adult from church or elsewhere that called to speak with me. To my parents, it seemed irresponsible to say I was going to do something and then not do it.

You see, my mom and dad came from a different time. Back in their day when you told people you would follow through on your commitment, it mattered that you did.

But, in my adolescent mind, I did not think about how my actions impacted the way other people thought of me. I had everything around me to help me keep my commitments too. I had a computer, notebooks, a phone in my bedroom, and at times, my friends around the corner from my house. So, I thought that I would get to them when I was ready or maybe when I remembered.

I have since learned that the mind is flawed: we cannot keep track of everything in our head. I also know that when you are immature, you think things and people will wait on you; I have also learned that is not true. People want to know that they are important to you, that you will get back to them, and that you do what you said you would do.

Whether I thought I had good intentions to do what I said, sometimes I let my feelings or my mood dictate my actions. How many times do you tell people things that you either do not plan to do or you think you will do but you do not hold yourself accountable to? What do you think that says about your character? And most important, how do you think people feel about that? Your words count. They count for what you represent, which may be how reliable you are, or even how mindful or mindless people may consider you to be. Which do you believe it is? And how do you want to be remembered?

When my mother and father were kids, they did not have the option of doing what they wanted to do when they wanted to do it. They had to do what their parents told them to do and when they told them to do it. I grew up in the era during the onset of MTV and slightly more liberal parenting. When I was growing up, more households had two working parents that were out of the home for long stretches of time and expected their kids to be somewhat self-reliant. Parents in the 80s began treating their kids with more collaboration than punishment and aggression, or at least that was the case in some households. My parents oscillated between authoritative parenting of the past and a nuanced parenting of the changing culture of the time. The purpose of that I suppose was to help me develop integrity and interdependence: traits I strive for in my present relationships.

I know we live in a climate where you hear people telling you not to care about what other people think. OK, I get the purpose for that. What they are saying is that you should do brave things without indulging in what other people's opinions are about it. That is different. And that is not what I am saying here. Instead, the things you commit to add up. It will add up in the ways that people think of you when great opportunities arise. It will add up in the ways in which your habits will leave a lasting impact on others. It will add up in the ways it will affect your income,

your health, and every other aspect of your
life. It all adds up.

As you age, your most meaningful
relationships will come from people who have
a high regard for your identity. How does that
begin? One way is by the way you respect the
things that come out of your mouth followed
by the things you do repeatedly. For every self-
help book I have read, to every life coach and
guru I have discovered, they all say to align
your words with your actions. Do that over and
over and over again. Gary Vaynerchuck, the
author and serial entrepreneur who wrote the
bestselling books *Crush It* and *Crushing It!*,
is on social media every day teaching people
how to do just what I am talking about here.
It is no different than your parents telling you
the same thing. But, of course it is easier to
take advice from someone we do not see, talk
to, or live with every day. The people who live
a principled life or seek to learn how to live a

principled life do so by creating reminders in people's minds of who they are.

Today, I thank my mom and dad for instilling that lesson in me. To repeat here a saying that my dad used to say repeatedly: "If you say you're going to do something, do it! If you change your mind, say so." It was really that simple. In different ways, the message I received from my parents was to be honest with myself and thereby be honest with other people. They were helping me to build character; and for that reason, I have been a part of some of the most meaningful experiences with others, and I have healthier relationships with myself and those closest to me. Happy people, people with high emotional intelligence and people who are remembered for great things, are people with integrity.

* * *

The question to put on replay in your head is, Who do I want to be, both to myself and to other people in this life? Begin by asking this question of yourself as often as possible. If you do not like how you currently function in the world, rethink who you want to be. Every time you start wavering because you did not get the results you were looking for right away, continue doing the thing you said you would do. Commit to the commitment. Even without the verbal validation from others, pay close attention to how you feel about it first. Then, watch how people start to respond to you showing up in your life because you made your words count by being present with your commitments. It all adds up!

No Matter What

In the last chapter, I talked about having integrity and not letting your feelings or your mood dictate how present you should be with your words and your actions. Well, now I want to share with you how building that foundation can pay off.

When I started writing this book, I was recovering from a tumultuous year of losses and gains, which is the flow I am usually in from one year to the next (I will explain more in a moment). However, the way I thought about what I was gaining far outweighed sometimes the things I lost. So, when I signed on with my publisher to write this book, I had decided that this was the time to do it. Was it the most ideal time for me? I would say maybe not. But, then again, I knew if I did not say yes at the time I was approached, I would have probably not written *this* book at all.

Let me take you back for a second to the top of 2019. It began with an amazing trip to South Africa, one of my favorite places on earth. It was the birthday trip of my dreams, and it came with lots of surprises, starting with the car I dreamed of being driven to my hotel in. It was a black Mercedes-Benz E-Class with a gracious driver, who told me a little more than I knew about the eleven languages he spoke. I spent five days in Johannesburg, relishing in the beautiful and abundant greenery the country offers, as well as indulged in lots of small talk with the kind people from the area, ate delicious foods, got the rest I so desperately needed, and of course spent some time sightseeing. I visited the

Nelson Mandela Museum as well as the last mansion he lived in before his demise, and spent a day in Soweto, a humble place filled with a powerful rebellious history. When I returned to New York, I was ready to begin expanding my online presence with work as a life coach, psychotherapist, and speaker.

Ironically, just as I was starting to feel the benefits of my time away, my family started going through changes. I experienced five deaths in six months, beginning with a beloved grandfather the first week of March, then an untimely death of one of my sister's two weeks later, the death of my father's youngest sister, another beloved grandfather, and finally the fifth and most significant death in early September with my father. I could not have planned for this amount of bereavement, but there I was having to make funeral arrangements with my family for my dad while continuing to run my small business and speak to people about their mental health needs.

Meanwhile, I surprisingly held up well with my grief while at the same time my business was accelerating. I recognized later that it was the continuous spiritual work I had been doing that year that helped get me through these losses. I had started listening to podcasts and reading articles on death and dying and having conversations with people in my life about it. By the time my dad took his final breath at home in bed, I was standing outside of a funeral home in Harlem, waiting for the doors to open to the place where I was about to lay his sister to rest.

Leading up to those days of letting go, I began developing a different outlook on death. Of course, I never could have predicted the way those circumstances occurred, nor as close together as they did, but being mindful of where I was moment to moment tremendously helped ease the pain. I continued to reflect on how my feelings and what I could learn from them, as well as how I wanted to live my life more fearless than before.

I have been a mindfulness practitioner for approximately three years. It has been the greatest intangible gift I have ever discovered. Being nonjudgmentally aware of what I am thinking and feeling, and how I am relating to myself, other people, and my surroundings, gives me an internal and an external level of awareness. I breathe through every moment and look at what I am grateful for and in what ways I need compassion and love. I learned an incredible lesson about grief: do something meaningful with it. As author and speaker, David Kessler (2019) calls the sixth stage of grief *finding meaning in loss*, which is exactly what living fearlessly is all about to me. Everything—including expanding my company's services, creating a digital footprint, and even writing this book—has been about living with meaning.

Years ago I started thinking about the intentional ways I wanted to live more abundantly, and after coming up with a few ideas, such as spending purposeful weeks each month with my parents, traveling the world more often, and not only saving but also making more money, life has overall been really good to me.

Do you remember when I stated in earlier chapters that everything is not about you and that committing to your commitments will pay off? Well, these past few years have tested the hypothesis that if I do what I say and show up where I can, when I can, repeatedly, the benefits would greatly unfold.

Between 2018 and 2020 people have asked me to consult on paid projects, such as the one I was referred to in late 2018 for Arianna Huffington's company, Thrive Global (TG).

It was through working with a partnership between TG and another company that I was able to serve employees using mindfulness as an antidote to workplace burnout. Lately, I have been consulting on a project helping black birthing parents through PTSD. And in recent months, clients have called my office saying that they were recommended to me because of a friend who knew about my work or that they saw me on a show discussing mental fitness and well-being.

Two years ago, after I was awarded a community plaque for my dedication to serving others, I went out to dinner with a group of people who were members of the organization that presented the award. As I was explaining to a gentleman what I do, he asked if I would be taking insurance. My answer was no. What he said next propelled me to go after my dreams even harder. He retorted, "That won't work! It's not sustainable. People aren't going to pay you out of pocket for services."

What he said was something I had heard all my life: doubt. I was used to it already. That same negative thinking made me hungrier. That night I left the dinner more inspired and more ready than ever before. I wanted to solve the problem. The problem was not that people would not pay me for what I do, because they already were. I was not necessarily getting the exact amount I wanted from all of my work, but I was content with my growth. Still, I wanted to solve the problem of how to get people to pay me my worth. The answer to that came in a few ways.

Within a year and a half of making the decision to go into full entrepreneurship, I began connecting to media brands and outlets who were looking for someone like me, a young professional who could speak confidently about mental health and entrepreneurship. Saying yes a lot in the beginning helped me become more visible, thereby memorable in my industry. I committed myself to becoming more fearless. Everything I did was about raising my value and putting my work in front of people. I knew I wanted to create a legacy, so I also began adding different things to the cultural landscape about wellness that few practitioners were talking about.

It is important to state that I had help along the way. People were willing to help me grow my business and also support my online presence, which at the time mostly consisted of me posting inspirational messages on Twitter and Instagram. As I expanded my reach, I started a podcast, hired a publicist and an assistant, and narrowed in on branding myself. Around this same time, I took a colleague's advice to join a professional service directory so that I could target the clientele that I deeply desired working with. I was scared at first. I had already tried that, but I did not get any good hits. My colleague said, "Try again." I waited. Then I went to her profile, read her bio, and saw how she positioned herself, and voila, I was back online, with higher rates and much more appealing working relationships.

I did not stop there. I also evaluated my environment and my friendships. What I noticed was how unsatisfied I was with some of my friendships. Just as I had set non-negotiables in my business, I had to establish better standards for the kinds of people I wanted to know. I had done this in my career and was enjoying the fruits of my labor, so why not experience abundance everywhere else? After years of therapy, mindfulness practice, and meditation, I came to the realization that I was tired. I was tired of the one-sided ties to people I cared about. I was tired of feeling fatigued from giving my time, my energy, and my attention to people who rather talk a lot about themselves than to be a present or thoughtful friend. And I was tired of being mad about it, too. I had to decide what type of people I wanted to grow with, support, and be supported by in order to feel as loved and cared for as I love and care for others.

As I began loving the life that I designed for myself, which began with accepting the life I was given and then choosing to live purposefully, I also started to gain confidence in my abilities, my talents, and my life's work. Ultimately, I developed a "no matter what" attitude about prosperity and joy.

Today, I know that no matter what, life will have its ups and its downs, but I also know that no matter what, I did not get this far on my own without a lot of lessons learned. It took the love of my parents, who did the best they could with what they had. And what I did not get from them I got from other people. Now I give what I need to myself. No matter what, it is your duty to yourself to at least get out of this life what you hope for — to give to it all that you've got. Just remember that there is no better life to live than the one you design for yourself.

CONCLUSION: KEEP GOING

I did it! I did exactly what I first came to do with this book, thus far. I wanted to share parts of my story of becoming the person I am today—an ambitious entrepreneur, a small business owner, and a transformational exhibition of all things prosperous! It was not easy. When I started writing this book at the turn of a new decade, I began to hit roadblocks directly in the middle of my writing. I was working with my clients, traveling abroad and domestically, and creating space for a new relationship shortly before the world turned on its head with the coronavirus pandemic. Practically every week since the beginning of spring, I encountered a crisis. Either a client's loved one would test positive for the virus or would personally get infected, most times, falling gravely ill. I felt concerned about my clients and fatigued, working to keep up with my professional life as well as my home life.

Still, I made a commitment. I committed to offering practical, actionable steps and questions to have you reflect on how you can live a life that is bountiful and happy. I wrote this book to transform lives. I want you to feel the words lifting off these pages and touching your soul, because that is how much I believe what I have shared can guide you into leading your life from the driver's seat, not the backseat.

This book has truly been a labor of love and courage. It scared me every day to pen the words to the paper, but I did it. The more patient I became with myself, the easier it was to let the words flow. May you also build patience with yourself and gain confidence by repeatedly doing what you are good at, and then in every way valuing yourself, valuing your life's work, your relationships, and your health. Whatever you do, keep going—it all adds up.

Appendix:
Recommended
Reading List

Brown, Brené. *Men, Women, and Worthiness: The Experience of Shame and the Power of Being Enough.* Read by author. Louisville, CO: Sounds True, 2013. Audiobook, 2 hours and 14 minutes.

Cardone, Grant. *The 10X Rule: The Only Difference between Success and Failure.* Hoboken, NJ: Wiley, 2011.

Groins, Jeff. *Real Artists Don't Starve: Timeless Strategies for Thriving in the New Creative Age.* New York: HarperCollins Leadership, 2017.

Keller, Gary W., and Jay Papasan. *The ONE Thing: The Surprisingly Simple Truth Behind Extraordinary Results*. Austin: Bard Press, 2013.

King, Shaun. *The Power of 100!: Kickstart Your Dreams, Build Momentum, and Discover Unlimited Possibility*. New York: Howard Books, 2017.

Ruiz, Don Miguel. *The Four Agreements: A Practical Guide to Personal Freedom* (A Toltec Wisdom Book). San Rafael, CA: Amber-Allen Publishing, 2018.

Ruiz, Don Miguel. *The Mastery of Love: A Practical Guide to the Art of Relationships* (A Toltec Wisdom Book). San Rafael, CA: Amber-Allen Publishing, 1999.

Vaynerchuk, Gary. *Crushing It!: How Great Entrepreneurs Build Their Business and Influence—and How You Can, Too*. New York: Harper Business, 2018.

References

Keller, Gary W., and Jay Papasan. 2013. *The ONE Thing: The Surprisingly Simple Truth behind Extraordinary Results*. Austin: Bard Press.

Kessler, David. 2019. *Finding Meaning: The Sixth Stage of Grief*. New York: Scribner.

About the Author

Asha Tarry is an award-winning community mental health advocate, psychotherapist, and certified life coach. Her career has been focused on the needs of people in oppressed communities and on international professionals in the workplace. She is a public speaker, writer, and activist, and in her spare time she enjoys traveling, partaking in ethnic cuisines, spending quality time with loved ones, and continually developing her spiritual lifestyle practices.

For more details on Asha's work, go to www.LifeCoachAsha.com for life coaching services, for speaking engagements, or to subscribe to her weekly blog where she provides coaching on transformational living.